HEBREW ILLUMINATIONS

HEBREW ILLUMINATIONS

ADAM RHINE

with

LOUISE TEMPLE

SOUNDS TRUE
Boulder CO 80306

© 2006 Adam Rhine

Printed in China

Rhine, Adam.
      Hebrew illuminations
      ISBN 1-59179-345-9
      Library of Congress Control Number 2006925110

TABLE OF CONTENTS

FOREWORD

BY RABBI DAVID ZELLER

It is indeed illuminating to see how far the Hebrew letters have traveled around the world and into the cosmos. It is a wonder how they have inspired people of many religions, traditions, cultures, and professions. What is this fascination with these strange shapes — the ancient, timeless, Hebrew letters? What leads one person to meditate on them in certain forms, another to illuminate them with inner meaning, someone else to create a Tai-Chi-like dance, another person to create yoga-like postures of the letters, and still another, our artist, Adam Rhine, to illustrate them in a totally different and enthusiastic manner, as we see them before us now?

I remember meeting the late Itzhak Bentov, scientific researcher and author of *Stalking the Wild Pendulum*. He talked about interviewing an Irish Catholic psychic who had traveled into realms far beyond the reaches of telescopes in observatories and space satellites. He reported seeing, with his mind's eye, strange shapes in the furthest reaches of being. Bentov asked the man to draw what he had seen. The shapes he drew — which he said made no sense to him at all — were shapes that Bentov knew only too well. They were the Hebrew letters!

Are they arbitrary ink blots and shapes randomly assigned to represent different sounds, like the "Just So" stories of Rudyard Kipling on how the leopard got his spots? Or are these mystical shapes generated by the sounds and vibrations they represent? Does the sound create the shape, or does the shape create the sound? Like an electric current flowing through a wire creates a magnetic field around it — or does the magnetic field create the electric current? Like shapes in magnetic filings generated by the magnetic field underneath them. Like the shapes of water crystals formed by sounds, vibrations, or thoughts, or the prayers and blessings said over them. What are these so-called letters?

Stan Tenen, of the Meru Foundation, has been researching the Hebrew letters for years. A mathematician, he originally had only the ability to read Hebrew letters from his childhood education, but with no understanding of the text. He was convinced that there had to be an ancient cosmic wisdom, and further, that it had to be stored in a safe place for all future generations. He felt the most enduring storage facilities were the ancient wisdom texts of the world traditions. Not knowing Sanskrit, Chinese or other timeless languages, he decided to start with the first verses in the *Torah*. Using the letter sequence of the Hebrew text of Genesis, in a three-dimensional field, he generated a spiral shape like a *shofar*, the ram's horn. This shape, when held at specific angles in front of a laser beam, produced the twenty-two letters of the Hebrew alphabet. He had found, encoded in the *Torah*, a pattern that could reproduce itself. His findings go on and on. He derived all this from the sequence of the first twenty-eight letters in the *Torah*. This was not about the meaning of the letters or their words—just their sequence in the words they formed.

What is more significant, the "visual" shape of the letter, or the "audial" sound of the letter, the numerical value, or its sequence? There are innumerable teachings and practices, ancient and modern, mystical and scientific, about these variations. There are many teachings and practices about visualizing individual letters or words or names of G-d. And there are other practices about sounding the individual letters, or the letters in G-d's name, with all the combinations of the vowel sounds with each letter, according to the teachings of the great kabbalist Abulafia.

And what is there to say about the name of each letter? English just elongates the basic sound of the name of each letter (how boring): Aaa, Bee, Cee, Dee, Eee, eF (aha—a letter whose name doesn't begin with its sound!), Gee, etc, etc. Whereas in Hebrew, each letter has a unique name, usually with a variety of different meanings and a numerical equivalence that adds even more to the inner meaning of the letter: *Aleph* (elevated, chief, #1), *Beit* (house, #2), *Gimel* (to bestow, camel, #3), *Daled* (door, lacking, #4), and so on.

Where does the numerical value of the letters, called *Gematria*, come from, and how does it "work"? Today, most countries and languages use the standardized numerals 1, 2, 3, 4, 5, 6, 7, 8, 9, 0, based on the decimal system, though there are other representations for the numbers. Roman numerals use some letters in various combinations to create numbers: I, V, X, L, C, etc. At the time of the ancient Hebrew language and alphabet, there was no separate set of symbols to represent quantity or numbers. *Gematria* wasn't an afterthought to impose numerical equivalence on letters to create more meaning. Simply put, in ancient Hebrew the letters were also the numbers. It was a decimal (base-ten) system where *Aleph* is also the number 1, *Beit* is 2, *Gimel* is 3, and so on through *Tet*, which is 9. *Yud* to *Tzade* is 10, 20, 30, etc., to 90. And *Kuf* is 100, *Reish* 200, *Shin* 300 and *Tav* is 400.

Someone reading the *Torah* could be reading numbers just as easily as reading letters. They are one and the same. And so it is quite natural to see the numerical equivalences, the *gematria*, of a word. "Love," *Ahava*, equals 13. "One," *Echad*, also equals 13. But one person cannot love without another person to love. And when we add up "love" plus "love," or "one" plus "one," we get 26 — which is the *gematria*, the numerical equivalence, for the four letter name of G-d, the ultimate representative of Love and Oneness. And so we see that the Hebrew words can take on wholly and holy different meanings that are literally built in.

The letters are actually comparable to the elements of the periodic chart in chemistry. Each letter has its unique qualities in its combination of lines (like the *vav*) and curves (like the *kaf*) and dots (like the *yud*). And the letters with their combination of shapes, sounds, and vibrations combine with one another to form words, just like the elements combine to form different molecules. According to Kabbalah, it is G-d's combining of the letters into words as He speaks that creates the physical reality of each of those words. *Abra Kedabra*, the magician's formula, is from Aramaic, the language of the *Talmud* and the *Zohar*, an ancient Hebrew dialect, that means, "I will create (*a-bara*) according to (*ke*) my word (*dabara*)."

Looking at the letters as the expressions of creation can bring us back to the creation, to G-d's dream and vision of the world that was intended to be, to the purpose of creation, and to our own seemingly unlimited potential for human creativity. As the process of creation recorded and encoded in the Hebrew Bible, the letters call our souls back to the *Torah*, to this Divinely generated text, and to the deepest secrets contained within the ancient teachings of Judaism.

Adam Rhine, an artist with a passion for studying the Jewish tradition, has chosen to "set" his letters, as it were, as jewels in holy text, understanding that they are so much greater than anything the human artist can portray. In the text accompanying the artwork in this collection, the letters are associated with Psalm 145, whose verses are arranged alphabetically. Many psalms are based on the alphabet and serve as a source of further understanding of the letters.

As you contemplate these letters now, go beyond the identified letter and its "sub-atomic" letter particles. Allow your imagination to soar and take you through the portals of these glyphs to the worlds beyond them. You might experience them changing like clouds, drawing you into your own interpretations. In this way they might function as mirrors. This is the nature of the contemplative process: we open ourselves to the stimulus — here, the bold and richly colorful illuminations of the Hebrew alphabet — and our inner being supplies the rest, taking us to previously unimagined universes within. The potential of art rooted in the sacred is to take us on a sacred journey on which we discover our own unique relationship to the Source of life.

The *Midrash* says that the *Torah* is the blueprint that G-d looks into as He creates the world. And I wonder if He had a sketch-pad, a doodle pad, that he sketched on before proceeding with the creation. The illuminated letters in this book are artistic, imaginative, personal expressions produced from his sketch-pad, as the artist, Adam Rhine, explains in his introduction. And who knows into what blueprint and into what future creative projects they will find themselves.

As you look to find the letters themselves within these very full tableaus, so may you begin to see the letters within the richness of the world around you. May you seek the letters in all their forms and mystery. May you seek G-d in all G-d's ways — in meditation, in sight, in sound, in the familiar and the strange, in yourself and in your neighbor — in all G-d's beauty. May the letters in this book spell out new directions for you to go in, new teachings to look for, and a new love for G-d and for G-d's incredible building blocks of creation.

ACKNOWLEDGMENTS

This book would never have come about without the vision and initiative of Tami Simon at Sounds True Publishing, along with the graphic design skills of Karen Polaski who pulled all the elements together to create this edition. Louise Temple added a richness and impact to the text that I could never have done alone, and Rabbi David Zeller contributed an enlightening forward.

A very special thanks to Leslie and Lawson Day at Amber Lotus Publishing, who were the first to take a chance on me and publish my Judaica artwork in their line of calendars. I want to include Claudia Montagner and Tim Campbell in there as well.

Going back a little in history, I thank my parents, two people who knew nothing about art when I arrived, for enabling me to pursue my dreams through private classes and four years of college.

No list of acknowledgments could ever be complete without thanking Karen C. Rhine, my loving wife and my toughest art critic. Nothing gets past her, nor would I want it to! From painting side by side in college to painting side by side in our home, I have become a much better artist over the years. Her painting skills and mastery of color are second to none, and they've had a powerful influence on my designs.

Beyond everything else, I thank Hashem, The G-d of Israel, for all the blessings bestowed upon me, the ability to create art, and the opportunity to share what He inspires within me.

INTRODUCTION

And Moses said: "Show me, now, Your glory!"

*Hashem said: "I will let all My goodness pass before you;
I will proclaim the name of Hashem before you, and I will favor when I wish to favor,
and I will have compassion when I wish to have compassion."*

*And Hashem said: "You will not be able to see My face,
for man shall not see Me and live."*

And Hashem said: "Behold, there is a place with Me; you shall stand on the rock.

*"And it shall be that when My glory passes by, I will place you into the cleft of the rock,
and I will cover you with My hand until I have passed by.*

*"Then I will remove My hand, and you will see My back;
but My face shall not be seen."*

Exodus 33:18–23

For me this interaction between G-d and Moses in the Torah explains not only the role of the Divine Presence in my own art and life, but in the creative works and lives of all people in this world — in our music, in our prayers, in holy matrimony, in the birth of a child, and in our final moments.

This book was over five years in the making. It was an absolute labor of love for me, a passion, and an obsession that drove me to paint all the imagery that flooded into me. Art to me ranks just below breathing, just above food, and way above sleep. Before and after my "day job," at which I push pixels instead of painting and write HTML instead of Hebrew, I used every spare moment to compose the paintings you now see before you. My only days of rest were the *Sabbath* and the *Yom Tovim* (holy days).

Not all my works and ideas turn out the first time, despite hours of valiant effort! Artistic frustration is part of the deal, and acknowledging this doesn't make it any more pleasant. As a young artist, I used to tear up paper or throw things around in my bedroom. As an adult, I focus my negative energies on more productive outlets like exercise, paying bills, or straightening up my studio space. And when the sparks of creativity return, there is nothing more thrilling than solving complex design issues of shape, color, and balance in a painting that's "working." It is not during the act of creating art, but long afterward, that I feel something larger than myself is at work. Be it an hour, a day, or even years later, this reality starts to become clear. The mystery of the creative process is alluded to in the *Torah* quote above.

The writing of this book was an altogether separate challenge for me. Though a picture is worth a thousand words, it's easier for me to paint the thousand than write the hundred. After completing the first draft, I was joined on the project by author Louise Temple. She immediately brought a surge of creativity and energy and a wealth of knowledge to this endeavor. After many delightful hours on the phone and dozens of drafts emailed back and forth, the prose was refined and elevated to what you're about to read. It was an honor to work with her, and her talent with words is a blessing to all who read them.

We have tried to approach the different appellations for the Divine with sensitivity and mindfulness of the human tendency to anthropomorphize and thus limit a more open perspective. There are seventy known Names with which to identify our Creator in the Hebrew language. They are all holy and are not traditionally used in non-sacred texts, such as a book of art. To honor this, I made the decision to use "Hashem," which means "The Higher Name," and "G-d" without the vowel "o."

In the prayers of the Reform, Conservative, and Orthodox movements (and I've been involved in all three in that order), Hashem is identified as male. This is to instill both love and fear of a father figure Who judges our actions, protects us, and enforces discipline. Though The Holy One is accurately referred to as both "Our Father, Our King" on *Yom Kippur* and as the *Shechinah* (*Sabbath* Bride) every Friday night, we know that our Creator is One, without separate parts or needs or gender.

Hebrew Illuminations is to be enjoyed simply as an art book of abstract Judaica designs and illuminated Hebrew letters. The first section is comprised of watercolor paintings that celebrate each of the twenty-two letters of the Hebrew alphabet. Since childhood I have been fascinated with the beauty and calligraphy of Hebrew, not knowing the rich depth of meaning within each letter. Even during my teenage and college years, when I drifted away from my faith and heritage, Hebrew letters and words would pop up in my abstract paintings. It wasn't a conscious thought, they just had to be there. Hashem's hand was not seen, but looking back now, the message was unmistakable.

Hebrew is more than just characters on a page; it is the language of prayer and communication between Hashem and the Jewish people. This is the language used on the *Luchot* (two tablets) that the Lord wrote for Moses to bring down from Mt. Sinai. It has united our people for over 5,000 years in history, prayer, and song. Many enemies of the Jewish people have outlawed and burned Hebrew texts, knowing and fearing its importance, but it is alive today in the twenty-first century as it has never been before, being the spoken language of the State of Israel.

I have used Psalm 145, known as *Ashrei*, to provide a context to open our hearts to the letters. King David himself wrote the Psalm as an acrostic, as the first letters of each line are in alphabetical order. Each sentence poetically reveals insight into the letter that starts it. Recommended by our Sages to be read three times a day, *Ashrei* is a powerful and moving prayer that speaks of Hashem's involvement in the world created for us and our unending love in return.

The second half of this book features a selection of twenty-two of my ongoing *Magen* David (Shield of David) series. Let me try to share my ceaseless fascination and spiritual attachment to this shape as I describe my unusual approach to it as an artist.

I am a doodler. I started early in life tracing comic books until I could draw them on my own. At age eleven, I declared to the world (i.e., my parents) that I was an artist. Learning how to doodle covertly during classes, in narrow margins of homework pages and on the backs of notebooks with ballpoint pen, is a skill that has risen to a new level in adulthood. The instant the mood strikes, I start all my *Magen* David designs on stick-it notes or on pads of paper as 1"x1" tiny ballpoint pen sketches. Not only am I consistently surprised at how much detail can work in such a small area, but I have been able to draw literally thousands of *Magen* David ideas since 1999. Later, I cut out each image and glue it into my sketchbook.

When I sit down to create a new painting, I often open my sketchbook and flip through the pages. Having drawn so many ideas, it's as if I'm seeing many for the first time. At that moment, a design will inspire me as being *the one* to focus and expand upon. I usually don't remember when I did a particular sketch or what I was thinking at the time. But again, Hashem's work is not always obvious at the time of an event; only later can it be fully realized.

Now that I have my design, I will break out the rulers, compasses, and templates to redraw it much larger. More often than not, there are design issues that I didn't completely solve in the one-inch sketch, and so the real work begins. I am also able to add a lot more detail at this stage.

The facilitator is

My goal is to weave and overlap intricate shapes to create visual tension and intense beauty. When done effectively, the kaleidoscopic effect leads to an intangible connection to my own soul, and from there to my Creator.

Color is extremely important to my artwork, as it serves to infuse a design with energy and intensity. In the tiny black-and-white pen drawing, I can usually "see" the colors certain shapes have to be. It's an indescribable impression with no rules or formula, simply a feeling. As the sketch is fleshed out into its final, full-sized line drawing, I begin to work on quick color sketches with watercolor paint. Problems arise as the color choices I know to be absolute from the start leave me with an incomplete color map going into the final work.

Even without a fully planned color sketch, and because I am a very impatient artist, I go right to the final board or paper and begin painting. I will often literally "paint myself into a corner" when I've resolved all but a few portions. I'm suddenly left with unfinished areas that could ruin the entire piece! But I have faith in Hashem that I will eventually be inspired with a solution. In the meantime, I rely on the expertise and advice of my fellow artist and wife, Karen, with whom I've been blessed.

After my intense focus on the process of producing art, I look at my painting again as a viewer and not as the craftsman. It is only then that I see past all my labors and absorb it as a whole. I feel the impact my paintings project, far beyond the pencils, paint, and paper used to create them.

Hashem's face is hidden from us as we live our lives, work at our occupations, raise our children, and pray at home or in the synagogue. We rarely get a one-for-one pay-off after completing a *mitzvah* (commandment) or saying a prayer, and it can challenge our faith when we don't feel a sense of direct reward. But as The Lord told Moses, "… you will see My back," which is the moment we realize that for our positive efforts, we have indeed been blessed. Trying our best to follow the words of the *Torah*, doing our part to repair the world (*Tikkun Olam*), and doing good throughout our days does pay off in the method and time of G-d's own choosing.

I hope you continue to see and seek out the blessings that have been bestowed upon you and realize Hashem's continual presence in our world. You may find it in a child's smile, a sick person nursed to health, a recently married couple starting a new life together, and sometimes even in a simple little painting.

— Adam Rhine, Tevet 5766
January, 2006

HEBREW ALPHABET

אַשְׁרֵי יֹשְׁבֵי בֵיתֶךָ, עוֹד יְהַלְלוּךָ סֶּלָה.
אַשְׁרֵי הָעָם שֶׁכָּכָה לּוֹ, אַשְׁרֵי הָעָם שֶׁה' אֱלֹקָיו.
תְּהִלָּה לְדָוִד

Ashrei yoshvei vei-techah, od ye-hallel-uchah selah.

Ashrei ha-am sheka-chah lo, ashrei ha-am sheh-Hashem elo-kav.

Te-helah le-david …

Praiseworthy are those who dwell in Your house, and may they always praise You, Selah!

Praiseworthy is the people whom this is so, praiseworthy is the people whose G-d is Hashem.

A psalm of praise by David …

ALEPH

1

‫ארוממך אלקי המלך, ואברכה שמך לעלם ועד.‬

Aro-mi-mecha elokav ha-melech, va-avar-chah sheem-chah le-olam va-ed.

I will exalt You, my G-d, the King, and I will bless Your name forever and ever.

The letter *aleph* is the symbol of the unique oneness of the Creator. *Aleph* is one; G-d is one.

It is the letter that begins *Ashrei*, the name of this psalm ("Praiseworthy"), and the first word *Aromimcha*, or "I will exalt You." Exaltation is the orientation of our connection to and faith in the Essence of existence. *Aleph* also begins the word for "love"—*ahava*. This holy letter is composed of three parts: two letter *yuds* connected by the letter *vav*. The numerical value of these letters when added together is twenty-six, which is the same number comprising the letters of the most sanctified name of the Creator denoting love and compassion, the unpronounceable Tetragrammaton, spelled *yud-hei-vav-hei*. With the limited understanding of human intellect we cannot grasp the Infinite One, and yet, paradoxically, at the revelation at Sinai of the Ten Commandments, G-d addresses the Jewish people using the personal pronoun *anochi*, which begins with an *aleph* … "I (*anochi*) am the G-d, Your G-d, Who has taken you out of the land of Egypt …" This is a clear statement of both the transcendent and immanent in creation, and of the Creator's participation in the world and in our lives.

In the form of the *aleph*, the *yud* below touches the Earth and the *yud* above reaches heavenward, desiring to be close to Hashem. With the giving of the Torah, heaven and earth were united. Each of us can fulfill our purpose here by joining heaven and earth—revealing the hidden spirituality in the physical world—and by seeking to know the underlying unity, the oneness of reality. The mediating force of *vav*, upright like a human being, connects the two *yuds* into one entity. The *aleph* possesses the power to bear the polarity of opposites and of paradox.

May we find balance and harmony in this physical world as we honor and seek our source in the spiritual. In exalting G-d we stand strong and confident, knowing the true dignity of being human.

BEIT

2

בכל יום אברכך, ואהללה שמך לעולם ועד.

Be-chol yom ah-varche-chah, va-ah-halah sheem-chah le-olam va-ed.

Every day I will bless You, and I will praise Your name forever and ever.

Beit is the first letter written in the *Torah.* It starts the word *bereshet,* which means "in the beginning." It also begins the word for blessings, *berachah.* We learn from this that there is a connection between beginning and blessings. The Creator of life generates life every second; therefore every moment is a new beginning and every moment is a blessing. As King David models for us, "Every day I will bless you ..." or *"Bchol yom avorecha ..."* From this we can take on the daily practice of developing and expressing a positive state of awareness. G-d blesses His creation, and creates it, with the attribute of loving-kindness, the attribute of Abraham, who is entrusted, as the first Jewish soul, with the Divine power of blessing.

Having a solid foundation, the letter *beit* represents a house or home. Each of us can be a home for the divine and a source of blessings to the world, making it a true home for the Divine. The value of *beit* is two, reminding us that the world is comprised of pairs: man and woman, day and night, holy and secular. This world of duality exists within the Source of Oneness.

May we find comfort and blessings in the place we call home, and find that which makes us complete and at peace. May we know that each breath is a new beginning and a source of blessing.

GIMEL
3

גדול ה' ומהלל מאד, ולגדלתו אין חקר.

Gadol Hashem oom-hu-lal, meh-ohd, veh-leeg-du-lah-toh ayn chay-ker.

Hashem is great and highly extolled, yet inscrutable is G-d's greatness.

Here *Gimel* is the first letter of the word *gadol*, or "great." Sometimes luminaries and scholars are called by this term, and yet nothing we can conjure conceptually, in human terms, can even approximate the vast greatness of the Creator of all existence.

The letter *gimel* contains within it a great force and power. It also begins the words for "strength," *gevurah*, and "might," *gibor*. Its shape resembles a body (*vav*) with the attached *yud* as a foot extended to the left. We can see this as a person running to give charity to the poor, thus fulfilling the will of G-d in one of the great acts of kindness entrusted to us. In this way we emulate G-d's continuous and loving generosity toward us.

Gimel's numerical value of three evokes our forefathers (Abraham, Issac, and Jacob), Hashem's presence in the holy matrimony between a man and a woman, and the three parts of the holy *Torah:* The Five Books of Moses, the Prophets, and the Writings.

May we always recognize that the source of true greatness and strength in this world is derived from the One Infinite Being. True greatness comes from knowing this.

DALED

4

דור לדור ישבח מעשיך, וגבורתיך יגידו.

Dor leh-dor yeh-shabach ma-ah-seh-chah, oog-vu-roh-techah ya-gey-du.

Each generation will praise Your works to the next, and of Your mighty deeds they will tell.

Daled begins the word for "generation" in Hebrew—*dor*. The eternal wisdom of the *Torah* is faithfully cherished and upheld through time, passed from generation to generation, bearing witness to G-d's greatness.

Daled also begins *delet*, for "door," *dirah*, denoting G-d's earthly dwelling, and *da'at* for "knowledge." The shape of the letter, with its horizontal top extending to the left of the vertical post, reminds us of a doorframe with one side open.

We learn that only those who are humble in spirit, who know that everything comes from G-d, can enter the door of the Divine Palace. The *daled* suggests the shape of a bowing figure and reminds us that we are all servants of the Sovereign Ruler of this universe.

Daled's numerical value of four reminds us of the four letters of the Holy One's unpronounceable name. There are also four matriarchs of the Jewish people: Sarah, Rivka, Leah, and Rachel. At the Passover *Seder*, four cups of wine are drunk, and the Four Questions are asked by the youngest child.

May we be ever-mindful of what we have been given, what we are being given right at this moment, and what we are passing on to those who will come after us. May we be worthy to seek out and pass through the doors of knowledge and understanding of the Commandments so that we can make this earth a spiritual dwelling place for Hashem.

HEI
5

הדר כבוד הודך, ודברי נפלאתיך אשיחה.

Hah-dar ke-vod ho-deh-chah, veh-deev-ray neflo-tech-chah ah-see-chah.

Let me speak of the splendor of Your power and Your wondrous deeds.

Hei opens this line with the word *hadar*, "splendor" or "glory." This can also be referred to as hidden beauty, to which we are drawn and attracted.

The soul, we learn, possesses three means of expression, or "garments": thought, speech, and action. The shape of the *hei* corresponds to these garments — the upper horizontal line to thought, the right vertical line to speech, and the unattached foot to action.

In all areas of the soul's expression we aspire to cultivate an inner radiance or brilliance that will reflect the glory of G-d. Aaron, the *Kohain Gadol*, "High Priest" and brother of the Prophet Moses, elevated the souls of those who had transgressed in the proper use of the soul's "garments." Therefore he represents *hod* (a derivative of *hadar*), a channel of divine flow in the *Kabbalah* system of ten emanations. So humble and pure was he that G-d's splendor could shine out fully through him, transforming with love those who had erred.

We can also see the *hei* as comprised of the letters *daled* and *yud*. The *daled* forms the right side, acting as a door to the physical world, and the *yud* on the left denotes spirituality entering our lives. Moreover, the letter *hei* appears twice in G-d's Holy Name, the Tetragrammaton, as if mirroring itself.

As we reflect upon this letter may we be reminded of another word, *hinani*, or "Here I Am," a declaration made without hesitation by Abraham, Jacob, and our teacher Moses, when called directly by Hashem. Here I am to do Your Will, to serve You with all my heart and soul. May I connect my thoughts, speech, and actions to You so that Your splendor will shine through me all the days of my life.

VAV
6

וְעֱזוּז נוֹרְאוֹתֶיךָ יֹאמֵרוּ, וּגְדוּלָּתְךָ אֲסַפְּרֶנָה.

Veh-eh-zuz nor-oh-techah yo-may-ru, og-du-la-techah ah-sap-renah.

And of your wondrous works, the people shall speak, and Your greatness they shall relate.

Vav means "and" when placed at the beginning of a word. The first *vav* found in the Torah is in the opening line of the Book of *Bereshet* (see the letter *beit*) where we read, "In the beginning G-d created the heavens and the earth." We learn that the very first time a letter or word is found in the holy *Torah,* that is its spiritual headquarters, so to speak. Here *vav's* essential purpose is to join spirit and matter, heaven and earth, body and soul. Standing upright like a person or a pillar, its hook-like shape connects concepts, or spiritual domains. It is also one of the four letters of the Tetragrammaton, G-d's Holy Name.

The numerical value of *vav* mirrors the manifestation of the six days of creation, the descent, as it were, of spirit into matter. The *Talmud* consists of six "orders," each containing the tractates that deal with a specific area of *Torah* law. In the central prayer of Judaism, the *Shema,* there are six Hebrew words in the first sentence: "Hear, O Israel, Hashem is our G-d, Hashem is One." There are six directions in space to which we turn on the high holiday of *Succot* to wave the four species that symbolize the unification of G-d's Name: north, south, east, west, up, and down.

Just as the holy letter *vav* unites both words and worlds, may we humans, standing unique amongst created beings, comprehend the underlying connection between all of creation and the ceaseless exchange between spirit and matter, soul and body.

ZAYIN
7

זכר רב טובך יביעו, וצדקתך ירננו.

Zeh-cher rav tu-vechah yah-bee-ooh, veh-zed-kah-techah yeh-rah-nay-nu.

*A remembrance of Your abundant goodness they will utter,
and of Your righteousness they will sing exultantly.*

Zecher, or "remembrance," is the first word of this verse. We are commanded to remember the *Sabbath*, the seventh day and seal of creation, which commemorates completion and wholeness. The feminine presence of the *Sabbath* is called the *Sabbath* Bride, or Queen, and mystically signifies the marriage between G-d and Israel, the feminine aspect of the Creator being called the *Shechinah*. On this holy day, realms of the soul are elevated to new awareness. The peace or rest of the *Sabbath* day derives from the spiritual concept of completion— everything being in place for the purposeful work of the six days. We abstain from productive labor and submerge ourselves in meditating on the perfection of the Source of all that exists and all that will unfold in the ensuing week. The seventh day is the soul of the physical and secular week.

The number seven also evokes the seven lower *sefirot* in the mystical teachings of the *Kabbalah*, the commandments in the *Torah* that connect to multiples of seven—the Counting of the *Omer*, the Sabbatical and Jubilee years, and the seven shepherds of Israel (Abraham, Isaac, Jacob, Joseph, Moses, Aaron, and David).

The shape of the *zayin* is that of a *vav* whose head extends in both directions like a crown or scepter, reminding us that humanity is the crown of creation, created on the sixth day in the image of G-d, so that we may reflect on this Sovereign gift on the *Sabbath*.

As King David reminds us, may we always remember who we are.

CHET
8

חנון ורחום ה', ארך אפים וגדל חסד.

Chah-nun veh-rahch-um Hashem, eh-rechah ah-pah-yem oog-dal chah-sed.

Gracious and merciful is Hashem, slow to anger, and great in (bestowing) kindness.

Chayn is the word for "grace" from which the first word of this verse derives. *Chet* is said to be constructed out of a merger between the opposing forces of the letters *vav* and *zayin*, joined at the top by an arch. This presents the concept of the tension, or paradox, between the absolute unity of Hashem and the plurality of creation. The above verse reminds us that the Creator of this world is understanding and benevolent and mindful of these forces. The word *chessed*, denoting the attribute of loving-kindness, begins with a *chet*.

Chai, the word for "life," is spelled with a *chet* and *yud*. This combination unites the presence of G-d (represented by the *yud*) to our existence in time (*chet*). The numerical value of these letters is eighteen, multiples of which are often given in currency as charity, to remind us of the gift of life and the benevolence that we are required to emulate. The word *chaya* is the second-highest level of soul, referring to the Source of life and the life-force itself.

Chet is like an open gateway between worlds of consciousness. The number eight is connected to transcendence, as it stands outside the seven days of creation. It is connected to the concept of *Moshiach*, the Messiah, and also brings to mind the eight days of *Hanukkah*, which commemorate miracles that defy the laws of nature. It is a holiday on which we celebrate light, a way of seeing from a purified heart.

As we contemplate this holy letter, may we feel the grace that permits us to soar through the archway of consciousness while being fully grounded in our lives within the physical world.

TET
9

טוב ה' לכל, ורחמיו על כל מעשיו.

Tov Hashem lah-kol, veh-rah-chah-mav al kal mah-ah-sav.

Hashem is good to all; His mercies are on all His works.

Tov, the word for "good," begins this verse. At the beginning of creation the appearance of light is called "good" in G-d's eyes. Righteous beings are also described in this way, as they reveal the inner light and purpose of creation. They exist in this world but are not of it. They are conscious of the physical world in order to rectify it while being fully aware that there is nothing other than G-d. Through the service of the soul, all reality is filled with the Creator's infinite goodness, bringing harmony and peace to this world. This is exemplified by the last seventeen years of our father Jacob's life that are described as "good," the numerical value of *tov* being seventeen. He lived in the depraved culture of Egypt yet studied *Torah* incessantly with his sons, thereby creating a foundation of strength for the Jewish people to withstand the exile that was to come.

Tet is shaped like an open container or vessel with a flat, stable base. It signifies the space for potential, an open womb. There are nine months of pregnancy, and nine *sefirot* pour blessings into this realm of *malchut*, G-d's Kingdom on earth.

Even when we cannot understand the workings of this world, we know that there is a Master plan and that everything, however challenging and difficult, is ultimately for good. A person of faith believes in G-d's goodness under all circumstances. By reciting *Ashrei*, we create a positive state of mind that enables us to see and to embody this benevolence.

May we see with *ayin tov*, "good eyes," the goodness in ourselves and in each other, filling the vessel of *tet* with infinite blessings.

YUD

10

יוֹדוּךָ ה' כָּל מַעֲשֶׂיךָ, וַחֲסִידֶיךָ יְבָרְכוּכָה.

Yod-ooh-chah Hashem kal mah-ah-seh-chah, vah-chah-see-dechah yeh-vahr-chu-chah.

All Your works shall thank You, Hashem, and Your devout ones will bless You.

Yud is the smallest letter in the Hebrew alphabet and is contained in all letters and words, as if it were a seed, the first dot of creation. It is the only letter that is suspended and is the first letter of G-d's Holy Name, the Tetragrammaton. It is whole and not built from separate parts, which is symbolic of the Oneness of Hashem.

The power of ten resonates throughout Judaism. There are ten Divine channels, or emanations of light, through which the Creator continually brings this world into being, and as each word and letter contains the power of *yud*, each is a channel for Hashem's infinite light to enter finite reality. There are ten commandments and ten utterances of creation ("Let there be light … ," etc.). Abraham survived ten tests of faith, and ten plagues were brought by Hashem against the Egyptians. A prayer service cannot begin without a quorum of ten men.

We speak of the *pintele yid,* the dot of Jewish essence that is never extinguished and that will continue to survive even the hardest trials.

May we contemplate the nucleus of all life that is the *yud* as it hovers in a state of becoming, soaring upward as the Divine point of everything. May we never "miss the point."

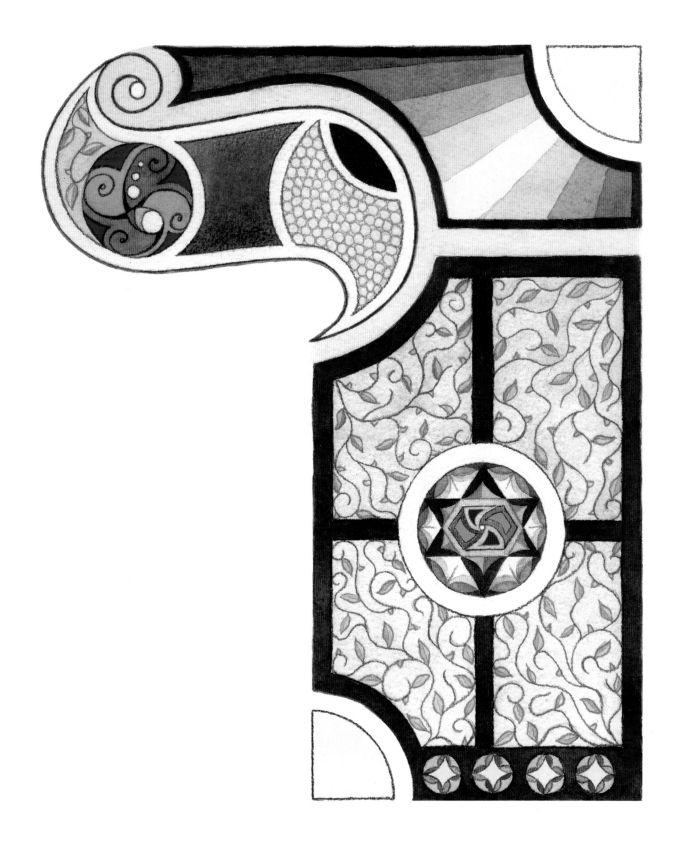

KAF
20

כבוד מלכותך יאמרו, וגבורתך ידברו.

Keh-vod mal-chu-techah yo-may-ru, oog-vu-rah-techah yeh-dah-bay-ru.

All shall speak of Your kingdom's glory, and of Your power they will relate.

Kaf holds the eleventh position in the alphabet and has a numerical value of twenty. Here it begins the word *kavod*, which means "honor," "glory," or "respect." It is incumbent on us to bring this attitude to all of G-d's creation and to the Source of all creation when we stand in prayer. *Kaf* is the first letter of the word *kavannah*, which means "intention," an essential preparation of the heart and mind before prayer, speech, and action.

Kaf is the root of *kipah* — a skullcap — and also means the palm of the hand. The shape of the letter has been described as a crown on the head of a prostrating king. It is not surprising that it begins the word *keter* or "crown," which is the highest of the ten *Sefirot*. The crown represents the Supreme Nobility of Hashem and a level of spiritual elevation beyond human comprehension. With this imagery we can relate to the skullcap as the palm of G-d blessing the head to fulfill its highest purpose.

Twenty appears in the Bible several times: Joseph's brothers sold him for twenty pieces of silver, Jacob worked for Laban for twenty years, and the maximum height of the *Sukkah* (the temporary dwelling we reside in on the holiday of *Sukkot*) is twenty cubits.

In honoring and respecting each other, we glorify G-d. May *kaf* remind us to purify our hearts and minds for prayer and meditation so we may receive the presence, the palm, of the Holy One.

LAMED
30

לְהוֹדִיעַ לִבְנֵי הָאָדָם גְּבוּרֹתָיו, וּכְבוֹד הֲדַר מַלְכוּתוֹ.

Leh-ho-dee-ah ley-venay hah-ah-dam geh-voo-ro-tav , ooh-cheh-vod hah-dar mal-chu-to.

To make known to all mankind, Your mighty deeds, and the splendor of Your glorious kingdom

———

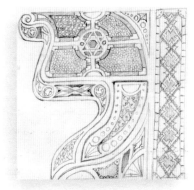

The literal meaning of the letter *lamed* is "to learn" or "to teach." In this verse it begins the word *l'hodiya*, "to make known." It is the only letter in the alphabet that ascends above the line, reaching up to the *yud* at its summit. This represents the aspiring heart that reaches up to receive the seed (*yud*) of wisdom from above. The Hebrew word for heart, *leiv*, also begins with a *lamed*, and this is the vessel into which consciousness is drawn to gestate. Our sages refer to the *lamed* as "a tower soaring in the air." In the study of *Torah* this alludes to our desire to grasp inner spiritual truth, transcending our earthbound nature and constantly aspiring to uplift ourselves and "make known …Your mighty deeds." These deeds express themselves in the physical world when we perform acts of kindness and emulate G-d's ways. In this way we create a relationship between our inner and outer spiritual life, coming close to the divine Source in holiness and service, drawing heaven into earth and earth into heaven.

The numerical value of *lamed* is thirty. In the *Midrash* (rabbinical commentary), it is said that when a person reaches this age they can begin influencing the world. Up until then they are preparing by building their knowledge and character. There are thirty days in the month, thirty categories of *tzaddikim* in the world-to-come, and thirty generations from Abraham to the destruction of the first Temple.

The *Torah* ends with a *lamed*, the last letter in the word "Israel." We all have the potential to reach this holy land inside and make known the glory of G-d in this world. May we stand tall like the *lamed* and strive for understanding every day of our lives. May we cultivate the wisdom of the heart, so our thoughts, speech, and actions make this world a "glorious kingdom."

———

MEM
40

מַלְכוּתְךָ מַלְכוּת כָּל עֹלָמִים, וּמֶמְשַׁלְתְּךָ בְּכָל דּוֹר וָדֹר.

Mal-chu-techah mal-chut kal oh-la-meem, ooh- mem-shal-techah beh-chal dor va-dor.

Your kingdom is a kingdom spanning all eternities.
Your dominion is everlasting from generation to generation.

Here, the *mem* begins the word for "kingdom"— *malchut*. We live in G-d's world, this physical domain, into which divine emanation flows and then rises like a fountain to flow back again. This is why *malchut* is associated with women, because it is the receptacle of divine plenty and goodness. It is the place of planting seeds, of "working the field," of birthing, and of creative manifestation. The shape of the letter *mem* is likened to the womb or a reservoir and is connected to the power of reproduction. The *mem* has two forms— open, and closed when it is placed at the end of a word. These two forms symbolize the revealed and hidden dimensions of the Torah. It is not surprising that *mem* begins the Hebrew word for "water," *mayim*, which is a metaphor for spiritual knowledge. All life depends on water. The Hebrew word for compassion, *rachamim*, ends with the three letters *mem-yud-mem*, the same letters that spell water. The word for "womb" in Hebrew— *rechem*— is connected to both *rachamim* and *mayim*, hence our understanding of the feminine presence in the Kingdom of G-d.

The number forty has great significance in the Torah. Moses ascended Mount Sinai for forty days, the Jewish people wandered for forty years in the wilderness, there were forty generations from Moses to the completion of the Talmud, the minimum quantity of water required for a *mikveh* (spiritual bath) is forty *seah*, the height of the entrance to the sanctuary of the Temple was forty cubits, and there are forty weeks of pregnancy. In the Jewish tradition it is believed that forty days before the birth of a baby, its soul-mate is announced in heaven.

Mem also begins the word *mitzvot*, the 613 divine precepts (or ways of creating a deeply personal, living relationship with Hashem) that are taught to us by Moses in the Torah.

May we always be open and receptive to the flowing Source of all life. As new seeds of awareness are planted and grow, may we always be open to change.

NUN
50

It is significant that the letter *nun* is omitted from *Ashrei*. In general, the *nun* corresponds in Torah to the image of falling, *nefilla*. This psalm is a prayer to instill in us, with every letter, a positive and elevated consciousness and to strengthen our faith and praise the Creator of all life with every fiber of our being.

The following letter, *samech*, means "support," the full embrace of the divine or, in other words, G-d's transcendent mercy. These ideas express the spiritual concept of the descent (fall) for the sake of the ascent. Every so-called mistake or act of forgetfulness can be a conduit for self-knowledge and a means to draw closer to Hashem. Thus, it is said, the *nun* does not appear but is supported by the *samech*. King David himself sings constantly of this battle with the forces of negation and of the ascent (the Psalms) to praise the glory of G-d. The numerical value of his name is fourteen, and *nun* is the fourteenth letter of the *aleph-beit*. The form of the *nun* is like a bowing servant, representing subservience and faithfulness.

The numerical value of *nun* is fifty, which represents transcendence. There are fifty gates of spiritual attainment, a cycle of fifty years culminates in the Jubilee, which is celebrated as a year of freedom in the Holy Land of Israel, there are fifty references to the Exodus in the *Torah*, and the spiritual practice of Counting the *Omer* between the High Holy Days of *Pesach* and *Shavuot* is fifty days.

Nun begins the word *ner*, "candle," and *neshamah*, "soul." We learn in the *Talmud* that "the soul of man is the candle of G-d." As we know, one flame can light up a room of darkness. As we contemplate the *nun*, may we reflect on the hidden source of light that is within all of us ready to illuminate this world and to serve our Creator.

SAMECH
60

סוֹמֵךְ ה׳ לְכָל הַנֹּפְלִים, וְזוֹקֵף לְכָל הַכְּפוּפִים.

So-maych Hashem leh-chal hah-nof-leem, veh-so-kayf leh-chal hak-fu-feem.

Hashem supports all the fallen ones, and straightens all the bent.

Samech is a complete circle, a metaphor for Hashem, the One who has no beginning and no end. All growth and evolution proceeds in spiraling cycles, as expressed in the symbol for infinity. *Samech* is an inclusive space, an enclosure that supports us, the divine embrace. The *Sukkah*, the temporary dwelling that we are commanded to reside in on the holiday of *Succot*, begins with a *samech*. It represents the *or makif*, the transcendent surrounding light that protected the Jewish people in the wilderness, described in the Torah as "clouds of glory." The *chuppah*, or wedding canopy, is also described as the *or makif*, as is the ritual of the bride circling the groom seven times. In a sense, the *samech* is the deep containment of holy intimacy. The wedding ring also conveys this in the union between two souls.

The emphasis *samech* has on its "center" is like the *Mishkan*, the "Tabernacle," in the desert around which the twelve tribes of Israel encamped and traveled on their journey through the desert. The Holy Temple was the center of religious life in Jerusalem, just as Jerusalem is now the center of Jewish identity through-out the world.

Sixty is the numerical symbol of an all-inclusive state; there were sixty ten thousands souls — 600,000 — that left Egypt in the Exodus, sleep is one-sixtieth of death, dream is one-sixtieth of prophecy, *Shabbat* is one-sixtieth of the world-to-come, honey is one-sixtieth of manna, and there are sixty tractates in the Oral Torah and sixty letters in the priestly blessing.

As we focus on *samech*, may we feel deeply at home in that place within that we call our center, breathing in the life-force that sustains us moment to moment, surrounded by the loving embrace of our Creator.

AYIN

70

עיני כל אליך ישברו, ואתה נותן להם את אכלם בעתו.

Ay-nay chol ay-lechah yeh-sah-bay-ru, veh-ah-tah no-tayn la-hem et ah-che-lam beh-e-to.

The eyes of all look to You with hope, and you provide them with their food in its proper time.

Ashrei celebrates Hashem's providential care—the Creator's constant watchfulness over every element of creation. Here, the letter *ayin* means "eyes," expressing the intimate connection between us and the Source of all that sustains us. G-d is all-knowing and actively present in every detail of our lives. How we surrender to this sense of Presence is the very nexus of spiritual practice and the way we conduct ourselves. Everything is infused with divine life, and since this is so, there is potential good in everything. It is asked of us to develop *ayin tov*, "good eyes," so that we may lovingly discern the spark of holiness in all that exists, particularly in our fellow beings and in all life that challenges us. In so doing, as King David reminds us in the above verse, everything becomes "food," a source of nourishment. How we look out into this world is how it is reflected back to us.

There are seventy Names of The Lord (according to the *Baal HaTurim*), seventy archetypal nations and languages, seventy Holy Days in the Hebrew calendar, seventy sages of the *Sanhedrin*, seventy years of King David's life, and seventy elders chosen by Moses.

The shape of the letter *ayin* can be seen as two eyes with optic nerves entering the brain.

May we see the Artist and Author in all things of beauty, in art and in nature.

May we see with the eyes of the soul, searching out G-d's goodness in everything, as we are lovingly watched over.

PEI
80

פּוֹתֵחַ אֶת יָדֶךָ, וּמַשְׂבִּיעַ לְכָל חַי רָצוֹן.

Po-tay-ach et yah-deh-chah, ooh-mas-bee-yah leh-chal chai ratz-ohn.

You open Your hand and satisfy the desire of every living thing.

Pei is the seventeenth letter of the *aleph-beit*, which is the numerical value of *tov*, or "good." In this verse it is connected to the word *poteyach*, "You open," and the concept of Divine generosity and beneficence. We are required to recite this verse with great concentration and joy, as it is a declaration of Hashem's universal goodness and caring for every creature.

Pei is shaped like an open mouth with an exposed tooth and is therefore connected to the power of speech, the oral communication of knowledge. It is said that wisdom proceeds from the inner eye of the heart to the mouth. The power of speech distinguishes us from the animal kingdom, for it is through speech that we express consciousness. Words can uplift, educate, and unite. They can also be weapons of disunity and destruction, G-d forbid. We are enjoined not to speak *l'shon hara*, "evil speech," and to diligently take on the spiritual practice of guarding our speech and using language to reflect the Divine image in which we are created.

Our teacher Moses was eighty when he led the Jewish people out of Egypt, received the *Torah*, and transmitted the Oral Law to the nation.

May our reflections on the letter *pei* instill in us a reverence for the gift of speech and the gift of life with which we have been entrusted. May we also recognize the merits of silence.

TZADHE

90

צדיק ה׳ בכל דרכיו, וחסיד בכל מעשיו.

Tzah-deek Hashem beh-chal deh-rah-chav, veh-chah-seed beh-chal mah-ah-sav.

Righteous are You in all Your ways, and magnanimous in all Your deeds.

Tzadhe is the first letter of the word *tzaddik* in this verse, meaning "righteous." Hashem is just and merciful in His judgment of us. This attribute is reflected in the spiritual "pillars" of each generation—the *tzaddikim*, or "righteous ones," whose saintly behavior elevates them—inspiring people to loving devotion to the Torah and its commandments. The righteous know Hashem in all His ways, in all the seemingly mundane activities and details of this world. Through their devout study and immersion in the spiritual precepts of the oral and written *Torah*, they raise the consciousness of the collective soul to higher levels of Divine perception.

The bent shape of the letter *tzadhe* symbolizes how the righteous humble themselves before the Lord, knowing from Whom their abilities and spirituality derive.

Tzadakah, the Hebrew word for "charity," begins with a *tzadhe*. It is often used synonymously with justice, truth, and kindness. Giving generously to those in need—family, neighbors, and the greater community—is considered righteous behavior and, in Jewish thinking, an act of justice. We follow the example of our righteous father Abraham, who ran to do acts of charity. We are not the owners of what we have been given, but the custodians. If we have been blessed with greater means than another, it is a sacred trust to be used wisely and in the service of those less fortunate. Through acts of benevolence that open our hearts to love, we grow closer to the Source and Bestower of all life.

Ninety is the age at which Sarah gave birth to Isaac, and it is the number of total consciousness. Ninety thousand elders danced before the holy ark when King David brought it to Jerusalem.

The symbol of *tzadhe* with its outstretched arms reminds us that giving and receiving are one, and that each of us has the potential to act from that place of the hidden *tzaddik* within.

KUF
100

קרוב ה' לכל קראיו, לכל אשר יקראהו באמת.

Kah-rov Hashem leh-chal ko-reh-av, leh-chol asher yek-rah-ooh-hu veh-eh-met.

Hashem is close to all who call upon Him, to all who call in truth.

Karov, beginning with the letter *kuf*, means "close." The idea of closeness with the Infinite One is hard to grasp intellectually and yet is the feeling tone of spiritual experience. We speak of an awakening (or an arousal) from above and of an awakening (or arousal) from below. Sometimes it is as if G-d is calling (from above) to us through creation, "Come close!" And sometimes it is our yearning for Truth that calls out, and this is a personal awakening in which the process of seeking is finding an ever-closer degree of closeness. The function of the *Korban* service (offering) in the Holy Temple was to eliminate the sense of separation between the individual who made the offering and Hashem. In offering up our limited selves at the altar, in surrendering to the Source of life, we grow close to our inherent holiness and to who we are meant to be in the image of G-d. *Kadosh* is holiness, also beginning with the *kuf*.

The descending *vav*, in the formation of the *kuf*, symbolizes the potential for unholiness, and the *kaf* shape, anchored on the line from above (the benevolent palm), is responsible for keeping the *vav* from descending completely.

Human temptation and the negative inclination are always present in our world. *Kuf* also means "monkey" in Hebrew. The nature of monkeys is to act on impulse and to imitate. They represent the restless, undisciplined aspects of human behavior that prevent us from coming close to our deepest selves.

One hundred is the age of Abraham at the birth of Isaac, one hundred is the life-span of the eagle, one hundred is the number of the daily blessings we say, and ten times ten is the perfection of the square. Nineteen is the ordinal value of *kuf*—the basis of the Jewish calendar is a nineteen-year cycle of the moon in relation to the sun.

Hashem is close. Come close! Listen to your calling! Call out and trust that you are being heard. Come as close as you can!

REISH

200

רצון יראיו יעשה, ואת שועתם ישמע ויושיעם.

Reh-tzon yeh-ray-av ya-ah-seh, veh-et shav-ah-tam yesh-mah veh-yo-she-aim.

The will of those who fear Him He will do; and their cry He will hear and save them.

In this verse of *Ashrei*, the letter *reish* begins the Hebrew word for "will," *rozon*. Every morning we pray, "The beginning of wisdom is fear of G-d." The word for "fear" in Hebrew, *yirah*, has many levels of understanding. Simply speaking, we can say that the *reish* is connected to the word *rosh*, meaning "head." When we aspire to connect our will to the Will of Supreme Intelligence, we open ourselves to receive wisdom. Thus "fear" is a healthy awe before that which is greater than us, and we use our *rozon* to elevate our state of consciousness. Further, the Hebrew word for "running," *ratz*, is related to *rozon*. We are asked to run to do someone a favor, to run to carry out Hashem's Will—the instructions, tools, or commandments He has given us to reach our potential as creatures created in the Divine Image. We learn that the natural state of the soul is to "run and return" between its Divine Source and physical reality. By aligning our will with G-d's, the soul affects physical reality. This is the pinnacle (*rosh*, "head") for which we can strive and the beginning (*reishit*, see the letter *beit*) of true intelligence.

The form of this letter is likened to a bowing head. We pray on *Rosh Hashanah* (the "head" of the year) to be blessed to act as the "head" and not as the "tail" in the coming year, that our highest selves will lead us in righteous actions.

The *reish* is the numerical halfway point of the *aleph-beit.*

In bowing in true humility, knowing our Source and our Beginning, may we be blessed to act upon this knowing, preceding all our actions and efforts with the prayer, "If it be Your Will …"

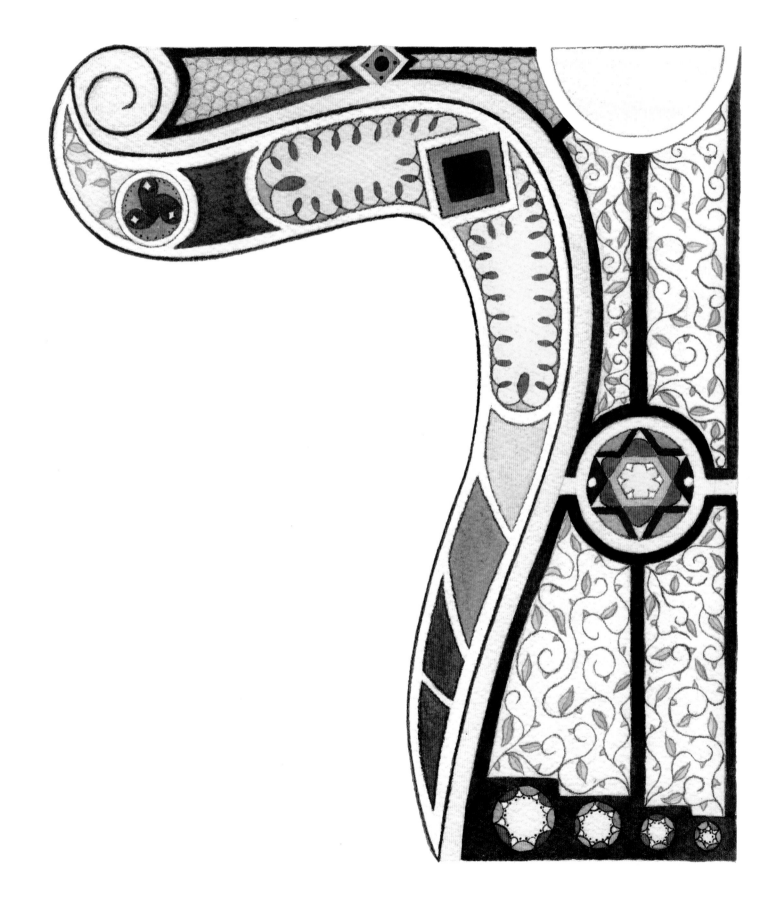

SHIN

300

שומר ה' את כל אהביו, ואת כל הרשעים ישמיד.

Sho-mayr Hashem et kal oh-ha-vav, veh-ait kal har-sha-eem yash-meed.

Hashem protects all who love Him, but all the wicked He will destroy.

The *shin* begins the Hebrew word *shomer* in this verse, which means "to guard," in the sense of safeguarding and protecting. The *shin* itself is a protection. It is written on every *mezuzah*, the prayer scroll that is affixed to every entranceway, and on the phylacteries that are bound on the arm and placed on the forehead of the Jewish male in prayer. The *shin* is the symbol for G-d's Name *Shaddai*, and is spelled *shin-daled-yud*, the attribute of the Holy One representing the concept of "enough"— guarding delimitations and boundaries. In a sense, it represents the gateway between the physical and spiritual worlds, the former being limited by necessity (or we would have no form) and the latter being limitless and infinite. As we enter our doorways and see the *mezuzah*, we are conscious of the Owner of this house, and by extension this world, and the One Who protects and guards us.

The form of the *shin* is three *vavs* rising like flames from a single base point. The flame is a symbol of love, as expressed in the above verse. The light of the Torah is seen as fire. In the candle flame we see three levels of light: the "dark" light around the wick, the white flame surrounding it, and the aura of the flame itself. There are three essential manifestations of love as taught by the *Chassidic* master, the *Ba'al Shem Tov*: the dark light corresponds to the love of Israel, that is, souls in physical bodies, the white light to love of Torah, and the aura to love of G-d. We can see the flickering flames of the shin as representing the mutability of all things, rising from an eternal, invariant Source.

These flames evoke the three patriarchs—Abraham, Issac, and Jacob—who tower for all generations in spirit, character, and courage, never abandoning their foundation in G-d.

Three hundred foxes were sent to burn the fields of the Philistines, the five letters of G-d's Name, *Elokim*, when spelled in full, equal three hundred, and there were three thousand parables of King Solomon.

We experience the *shin* in "peace," *shalom*, when we have complete faith that our well-being is watched over and that we are truly loved by the One who gave us life.

TAV
400

תהלת ה' ידבר פי, ויברך כל בשר שם קדשו לעולם ועד.
ואנחנו נברך יה, מעתה ועד עולם, הללויה.

Teh-he-lat Hashem ye-da-behr pei, vee-vah-raych kal bah-sar shaym kad-sho leh-olam vah-ed.
Va-ah-nach-nu neh-vah-raych Yah, may-ah-tah veh-ad olam, Halleluyah!

May my mouth speak praises of Hashem, and may all flesh bless the Name of the Holy One forever and ever.
We will bless G-d now and forever, Halleluyah!

In this final verse of *Ashrei*, King David speaks of praise or *tehillat*, the plural form—*tehillim*—being a name given to the Book of Psalms. David sang Hashem's praises even when battling great forces in himself and the world around him. How can we emulate this? The last letter, or seal, of the word *emet*, "truth," is the letter *tav*, which is the culmination of all the twenty-two letters, or forces, active in creation. We learn that Hashem's seal in creation is Truth. This is spelled out by the final letters of the last words in the account of Creation—*bara elokim la'asot*, meaning "G-d created to do." *Aleph-mem-tet* spells *emet*. These are also the beginning, middle, and end letters of the *aleph-beit*. The culmination of truth, when all is said and done, is simple faith, and this is the secret of the letter *tav* and of King David's ability to remain in a constant state of praise.

The form of the *tav* is composed of a *daled* joined to a *nun*, resembling a stamp or seal. Fittingly, *tav* begins the word *Torah*, the Five Books of Moses that reveal the light of G-d's wisdom; *Talmud*, the sixty-three volumes of the Oral Law given on Mt. Sinai with the written law; and the word for prayer, *tefilla*.

There were four hundred years of exile in Egypt and four hundred pieces of silver with which Abraham purchased the cave of *Machpelah* to bury Sarah. The dimensions of the Land of Israel are four hundred *parsah* by four hundred *parsah*.

As we experience the cycles of life, may we recognize with simple faith that the beginning, middle, and end of all things bears the seal of Truth. In believing in the underlying Perfection of all things we will be given the strength to "bless G-d now and forever, Halleluyah!"

MAGEN DAVIDS

SHEMA YISRAEL

Hear O'Israel, the Lord is our G-d, the Lord is One.

Devarim / Deuteronomy 6:4

The *Shema* is the most important prayer in Judaism. It is found in the Torah in Moses' final address to the Nation of Israel. It is said every morning and evening throughout the year and is inside every *mezuzah* scroll mounted on the doorposts of Jewish homes. The sentence itself declares that the Lord is One, and only One, whole and perfect.

My composition supports and illuminates the nobility of the statement, ornately framing the first two famous Hebrew words. I am constantly fascinated by the paradox between revealing the tiniest bit of G-d's splendor and beauty within a myriad of detail, and the nature of G-d Who is One and without "parts."

VALOR OF A WOMAN

An accomplished woman, who can find? Far beyond pearls is her value.

Proverbs 31:10

This design is inspired by the passage in Proverbs titled *Aishes Chayil*, written by King Solomon and read every Sabbath by a husband to his wife. The first three lines of the Proverb found in the painting read:

An accomplished woman, who can find? Far beyond pearls is her value.
Her husband's heart relies on her, and he shall lack no fortune.
She bestows goodness upon him, never evil, all the days of his life.

More than simply "valor" is implied by these words of deep, mystical meaning. The most straightforward understanding is that they are a testament to a woman who possesses the attributes she needs to carry out any task with virtue. *Aishes Chayil* is also a metaphor for the *Shechinah*, the feminine Presence of G-d, the "*Sabbath* Bride" who surrounds us on *Shabbat*.

To underscore the importance of the women of valor in our history, I have surrounded the composition with the names of the four Matriarchs (Sarah, Rebecca, Leah, and Rachel), the prophetess Miriam, and Ruth, the great-grandmother of King David.

I know my own life would be greatly diminished without the strength and love of my own wife, Karen. She is always at my side, through blessings and adversity, never afraid to speak her mind and never backing away from challenges. Her value is truly far beyond pearls, and no painting could ever capture how beautiful she is to me.

אשת חיל מי ימצא
ורחק מפנינים מכרה

בטח בה לב בעלה
ושלל לא יחסר

גמלתהו טוב ולא
רע כל ימי חייה

SHALOM

Grant abundant peace upon Your people Israel eternally, for You are the King,
Lord of all peace. May it be pleasing in Your eyes to bless
Your people Israel at every season, every hour, with Your peace.

Shalom Rav, Traditional Prayer

The word *Shalom*, meaning "Hello," "Goodbye," and "Peace," has deep significance to the Jewish people. We pray for peace, not only between the peoples of this world, but spiritually between ourselves and G-d. My painting depicts the two most important channels through which we can achieve peace in all ways. At top is the letter *yud*, the first initial of the Holy Name, and at bottom are the *Luchot*, the two tablets with the Ten Commandments. By looking to G-d above, and following the Commandments here on Earth, we will know how to conduct ourselves in holiness and establish peace wherever we go.

ZOHAR

The *Zohar*, "Splendor" or "Radiance," is one of the central books of Jewish mysticism, being a commentary on the soul of the *Torah*. It presents Judaism as an intensely vital religion of the spirit, a holy fire, as it were. The *Zohar* stresses that the spiritual forces above depend for their activity on the influences from below, that is, human thought, speech, and action. Thus, the thrust of my design depicts the intertwining of red flames from below with blue flames from above, as heaven and earth embrace.

ANI L'DODI, V'DODI LI

I am my beloved's, and my beloved is mine.

Shim HaShirim 6:3

This is from the "Song of Songs" written by King Solomon in the language of a beautiful, romantic declaration between a husband and wife, as an allegory for the love between the people of Israel and their Lord.

The intertwining beauty of love is captured in this painting by symmetrical designs reaching around each other, from the upper left and the lower right, embracing in spirals around the poetic center. Flora surround the union as the life of the couple grows and flourishes. The yellow circles, top, and bottom illuminate the warmth and light of G-d, blessing both sides in holy matrimony.

This painting was created as a *Ketubbah* (marriage contract), and the original is currently hanging in the home of newlyweds to remind them always of the sanctity of their marriage.

PESACH

... and now, go and I shall send you to Pharaoh, and you will bring forth My people, the Children of Israel, out of Egypt.

Shemot/Exodus 3:7

Pesach means "Passover" in Hebrew, the Festival of the Unleavened Bread that commemorates the Exodus of the Jewish nation, by the direct Hand of G-d, after more than two hundred years of bondage in Egypt. My painting is based on the unique plate that is used at the ceremonial meal, the *Seder*. The six positions of the different foods are, clockwise from the top, *Maror* (the bitter herbs), *Zaroah* (the shank bone), *Charoses* (a mixture of wine, nuts, and apples), *Chazeres* (the sweet herb), *Karpas* (parsley), and the *Baytzah* (the roasted egg).

The spiritual and ritual elegance of a *Seder* meal is found both in its order and its complexity, which I have tried to capture in my piece. The painting also contains a triangle motif, echoing the distinctive shape found in Egyptian architecture, desert sand hues, as well as a lush green border recalling the Nile River Valley.

TAL

Dew, precious dew—let it drop sweetly on the blessed land, with the delicacies of heaven sate us with blessing, to enlighten us from amid the darkness ...

Traditional Prayer for Dew

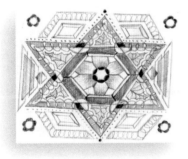

On the first day of *Pesach*, we pray to G-d for dew. The droplets, which remind us of the miracle of creation every morning, represent renewal and rebirth, teaching us never to take any blessing for granted, however small, like the dew on the earth. As the dew descends before dawn, it is a metaphor for the hidden secrets of the *Torah*.

The pencil sketch for this design was the second *Magen* David shape I ever put to paper. It sat in my sketchbook for over four years, not having a theme, until *davening* (praying) on *Pesach* morning. When the *chazan* (leader of the prayers) loudly chanted *"Tal!"* this design surfaced strongly in my memory, and the two were united. I now knew what the circles were in the four quadrants, and what their relationship was as dewdrops to the leaves in the center. The "Back of G-d" was again felt, in Hashem's own timing, by a gift of simple inspiration I will value forever.

CHAI

Each of the following three paintings was designed as a celebration of life, the greatest blessing our Creator has bestowed upon all of us. Each day of our life should be cherished and used to sanctify Hashem's Name, and to bring holiness to others, as we live on this beautiful planet. Each work of art was composed differently, just as we are all unique works of art in this world. The joy of a purposeful, *Torah*-filled life is represented in the ornate shapes and patterns, filled in with vivid and active colors.

GAN EDEN

And G-d took man and placed him in Gan Eden to work in it and guard it.

Bereshet / Genesis 2:15

––––––––––––

The Garden of Eden (*Gan Eden*) was a lush, floral paradise as described in the *Torah*. It was a place of incredible beauty and spiritual perfection where the Lord made every kind of fruitful tree grow, including the Tree of Life and Tree of Knowledge. My painting attempts to capture the pure and enclosed, whole, and holy environment from which humankind was banished, only to work on being worthy enough to return. In the center of the work is the letter *Gimel*, the first letter of *Gan Eden*, bursting out of yellow-green petals, filling the garden with G-d's presence.

YERUSHALYIM

May the Lord bless you from Zion, and may you look upon the glory of Jerusalem
every day of your life. May you see your children's children, peace in Israel!

Psalm 128:5–6

This is the name of the walled city in Israel, Jerusalem, which was reclaimed by King David, who set up the *Mishkan* (Tabernacle) and placed within it the Ark of the Covenant. David's son and successor, Solomon, then built the *Beit HaMikdash* (Holy Temple) on the very site where Abraham prepared to sacrifice his son Issac, and where Jacob had his dream of the ladder to heaven. This solidified *Yerushalyim* as the Jewish people's holiest city.

In my painting, calligraphic curves spiral and wrap around the Hebrew word *Yerushalyim*, as it is the center of every Jew's spiritual focus, no matter where we find ourselves. I have incorporated several *yud* shapes, emphasizing both the first letter of the city's name as well as the first letter of Hashem's Holy Name within a design that is intended to glorify the Divine centrality to the Holy City. As I drew, I was exploring curve upon curve within the confines of a geometric shape. Jerusalem, the holy center of the world, allows for the intertwining of such great diversity.

TZADDIK

The righteous shall flourish like the date palm, growing like a cedar in Lebanon.
Planted in the house of the Lord, they shall flourish in the courts of our Lord.
They shall still bring forth fruit in old age; vigorous and full of richness;
to declare that the Lord is just, my rock, in Whom there is no wrong.

Psalm 92:14–15

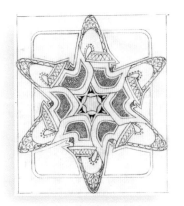

The Hebrew letter *tzadhe*, at the center of this Magen David, is the first letter of the word *Tzaddikim* or "righteous ones." This painting is dedicated to them, those individuals throughout history who have brought us the light of the Torah and of the Lord, and have spread blessings like far-reaching vines. Notable *tzaddikim* are our forefathers: Abraham, Issac, and Jacob (and their feminine counterparts, our Holy Matriarchs), Moses, Rabbi Akiva, Rashi, Rambam, and the *tzaddik* I read most frequently— Rabbi Moshe Chaim Luzzatto. This painting is dedicated to all those righteous ones who have been, and all those who are to come.

MISHKAN

The Lord spoke to Moses saying, "On the day of the first new moon,
on the first day of the month, you shall build the Mishkan, the Tent of Meeting.
There you shall keep the Ark of Testimony ..."

Shemot / Exodus 40:1

This was the portable sanctuary, or tabernacle, the Jewish people built and carried throughout their journey in the desert. The design of the outer rim that frames the six-pointed star was in my sketchbook for years, but the center remained empty. After studying the *parsha*, the *Torah* portion that describes G-d's specific instructions for the items to be used in the *Mishkan*, I created a *Magen* David design that combined the twelve-stoned *choshen* (breastplate worn by the *Kohen Gadol*), the Ark of the Covenant, and the seven-candled *menorah*. When eventually united with the outer rim design, the composition was complete.

I used a wet-into-wet watercolor technique to apply the colors, an homage to the cloud that would settle upon the *Mishkan* when G-d's Presence was communing with Moses and Aaron.

MAGEN DAVID DALED

By David, a psalm: Of mercy and justice do I sing;
unto Thee, Lord, will I sing praise.

Psalm 101:1

Daled is the first letter in the name of David HaMelech (David our King.) The six-pointed star is called the *Magen* David, or "Shield of David," since it was his standard. David wrote all 150 Psalms, songs to be sung by the tribe of Levi in the *Beit HaMikdash*, praising G-d's greatness. The letter *daled* is in the top point of this star.

This painting has a special place in my heart, as it is the very first Judaica painting I ever composed, setting the course for my entire *Magen* David series and all Judaica artwork to follow. It is also a rare occurrence when I am able to achieve everything I want in a design, from the almost-hypnotic depth of the geometry in the center to the color balance of the rust-brown background and the plum-blue tips. I had just turned thirty when I started focusing my art on Judaica and painted this image. For the interesting significance of the number thirty in relation to this fact, see the letter *Lamed*.

ALEINU

It is our duty to praise the Master of all creation.

Aleinu, Traditional Prayer

Written by the prophet Joshua after the fall of the city of Jericho, the *Aleinu* prayer is said at the conclusion of all three daily services, every day of the year. It declares the sovereignty of the Lord, the Creator of all existence, and our responsibility to give praise. It is recited standing up as we declare our faith, our fear, and our awe.

Aleinu has always evoked feelings of strength from within me. Declaring faith before G-d is empowering and complex, hence the strong, vivid colors and the spiraling interplay of shapes. As our devotion emanates from the center, the *Ayin Tov* is watching.

HANUKKAH

Hanukkah is a joyous eight-day festival that commemorates the miracle of the victory of the Jewish Maccabees over the Greek invaders of the land of Israel. The Greeks were led by Antiochus IV, the king who defiled the *Beit HaMikdash*, leaving only a small portion of oil for the *menorah*, enough for one more day. A miracle occurred, which kept the oil burning for eight days, the exact amount of time needed for new oil to be made.

I depict the *menorah* fully lighted at the bottom of the star, while the *shammus*, the center candle, is high above (just as it serves to light the other candles), projecting its light downward across the design. Since this is a time to celebrate the miracles in the history of the Jewish people, I added some joyful twisting and turning spirals for energy and motion.

TORAH

... the Torah of the Lord is perfect, it restores the soul ...

Psalm 19:8

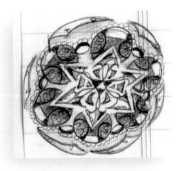

Who can paint the concept of *Torah*, the words of the Almighty, given to Moses on Mt. Sinai? For me, this painting is a celebration of the written covenant with the Jewish people, the unceasing assurance from the Source of all life and the fact that we are divinely protected and loved when we walk this ordained path. It is said that everyone has their own inner *Torah*, uniquely illuminated by the light of Truth as our lives "unscroll." This is mine—for now!

My spiraling design echoes the unceasing cycle of the reading of the *Torah*, year after year, generation to generation, as we wrap ourselves in G-d's holy words and decrees. In five of the circles are the five titles of the books: *Bereshet* (Genesis), *Shemot* (Exodus), *Vayikra* (Leviticus), *Bamidbar* (Numbers), and *Devarim* (Deuteronomy.) In the sixth and uppermost circle I put the crown of Hashem, the Supreme Author. When the *yetzer ha'rah* (evil inclination) surrounds and challenges us, we must look inward, into the core of our beliefs, to the beautiful blossoming rose of the *Torah*.

ISRAEL! ISRAEL!

Our Father in heaven, rock and redeemer of Israel, bless the State of Israel,
the first manifestation of the approach of our redemption.
Shield it with Your lovingkindness, envelop it in Your peace …

Prayer for the State of Israel

———————

This is my first painting to celebrate the reclaiming of the Promised Land by the Jewish people after almost 2,000 years in exile. The promise is that the *Beit HaMikdash* will be rebuilt in our time, and the *Moshiach* (Messiah) will dwell among us. I have used stone texture inspired by the Western Wall, the last remnant of the second Temple, and allowed its texture to recede into the distant center of the composition. Stripes of Israeli flowers cross to create yet another *Magen* David shape, with the Hebrew word for "Israel" on either side of the new star.

The tips of this *Magen* David are fragmented, broken off and floating in separate directions. They represent the Jewish diaspora, the breaking up and scattering of Jews in exile all over the world. These members of the twelve tribes will once again return to Israel and reunite in the land promised to the children of Abraham.

AHAVA

Praised are You O Lord Who has chosen the people of Israel with love.

Traditional Blessing

The last word of this blessing is *b'hava*, meaning "with love." The relationship we have with the Lord is based on love. The love we share is compared to the unconditional love between a parent and a child, and we are commanded to be mindful of this throughout the day, so we may be loving and tender to ourselves and to others. The people of Israel are chosen with love to be an example of G-d's love.

The composition for "Ahava" came about during a doodling session. Feeling uninspired, yet with the opportunity to draw, I wondered what a heart shape would look like inscribed in a *Magen* David. The rest of the design came together so fast I was stunned. With this painting I went for an obvious stained-glass effect. I also pulled in some of my favorite techniques from previous works: white dots on blue from "Zohar," vines and flora from "Ani L'Dodi," roses from "Yerushalyim," and alternating triangular tip designs from "Gan Eden." This is a work of love.

AYIN—EYE OF G-D

This painting emerged from a formless place, without words. The *ayin* is a silent letter, being a servant of the vowel sound it carries. It means "eye," which is a metaphor for Hashem watching over us, seeing our pure thoughts not clothed in words. The concept of *ayin sof* is Kabbalistic for the "great nothingness" or the unknowable Lord. When we annihilate our egos, so to speak, and return to "nothingness," then the Cause of everything can come forth. In this way it signifies the fullness of being that transcends being itself, for in this way we can reflect Divine Being. And because G-d's true nature is beyond our written or visual understanding, I have chosen a limited and subdued palette of colors to set up a vibration and a rotation around the center letter, *ayin*. I have attempted to express the paradox of the formless within form itself.

TIKKUN OLAM

Therefore we put our faith in You, Lord our G-d …
to perfect the universe through Your sovereignty

Aleinu, Traditional Prayer

Tikkun Olam is a Hebrew phrase meaning the "repair" or "fixing" of the world. It not only explains the Jewish idea of social justice, but also our highest purpose in making this realm a dwelling place for the Divine. The more *mitzvot* we do, that is, the more actions G-d has commanded us to do in order to express the Divine Will in this world, the closer the world moves toward perfection.

It is our duty to fix what we see as broken and bring beauty and harmony to our world. No individual is responsible for correcting every wrong on our planet, but each of us must rise in awareness to bring holiness to the people and situations we are able to influence.

This was one of the most challenging paintings of this collection. My original sketch included only the *Magen* David shape in the center. That's what I painted, and it turned out exactly as planned. My wife, a far better artist than I, saw the star floating by itself on the white board and commented that it looked unfinished. I agreed and began spontaneously to add everything you see around the *Magen* David. In its sketch-form, I had planned to make the theme *Ema,* or "Mother," but after I had completed all of the illuminated areas, it felt like a complete and beautiful world to me, hence *Tikkun Olam.*

ABOUT THE ARTIST

Adam Rhine is an artist who has been creating ornate, highly detailed Judaica watercolor paintings from his studio in Des Plaines, Illinois, since 1999. His style is greatly influenced by medieval illuminated manuscripts, which he combines with modern palettes and aesthetics.

Growing up an incessant doodler and cartoonist, Adam decided to pursue art at age eleven. He took private lessons from The Art Institute of Chicago Professor Alain Gavin, who exposed him to watercolor and oil painting techniques. He graduated with a BFA in Commercial Illustration from Northern Illinois University at age twenty-two, and was awarded the opportunity for a one-man show of sixteen abstract paintings in his senior year. He married his classmate Karen, a children's book artist, soon after graduation.

In his professional life, he has animated educational videos, coordinated the 2D/3D animation department for a video game company, created product illustrations, and executed Web site and e-learning development for large corporate sites. He is a member of the American Guild of Judaica Art.

Adam's intense imagery is featured in a successful line of "Hebrew Illuminations" wall calendars presented by Amber Lotus Publishing, who also produce Adam's line of Judaica greeting cards. His custom line of Hebrew Art Bar/Bat Mitzvah and Jewish Wedding invitations is available from Michael Gitelle Creations. Adam's distinctive Judaica art has translated into other media such as needlepoint canvases, cross-stitch charts, gift bags, Sukkah banners, Jerusalem stone/glass engravings, and even full-color Kosher chocolate candies!

The entire portfolio of Adam Rhine's Judaica images and products is on his own Web site, www.HebrewArt.com.

ABOUT SOUNDS TRUE

Sounds True was founded in 1985 with a clear vision: to disseminate spiritual wisdom. Located in Boulder, Colorado, Sounds True publishes teaching programs that are designed to educate, uplift, and inspire. With more than 550 titles available, we work with many of the leading teachers, thinkers, healers, and visionary artists of our time.

For a free catalog of wisdom teachings for the inner life, please contact Sounds True via the World Wide Web at www.soundstrue.com, call us toll-free at 800-333-9185, or write

The Sounds True Catalog
PO Box 8010
Boulder CO 80306